ALL DOGS HAVE ADHD

KATHY HOOPMANN

Jessica Kingsley Publishers
London and Philadelphia

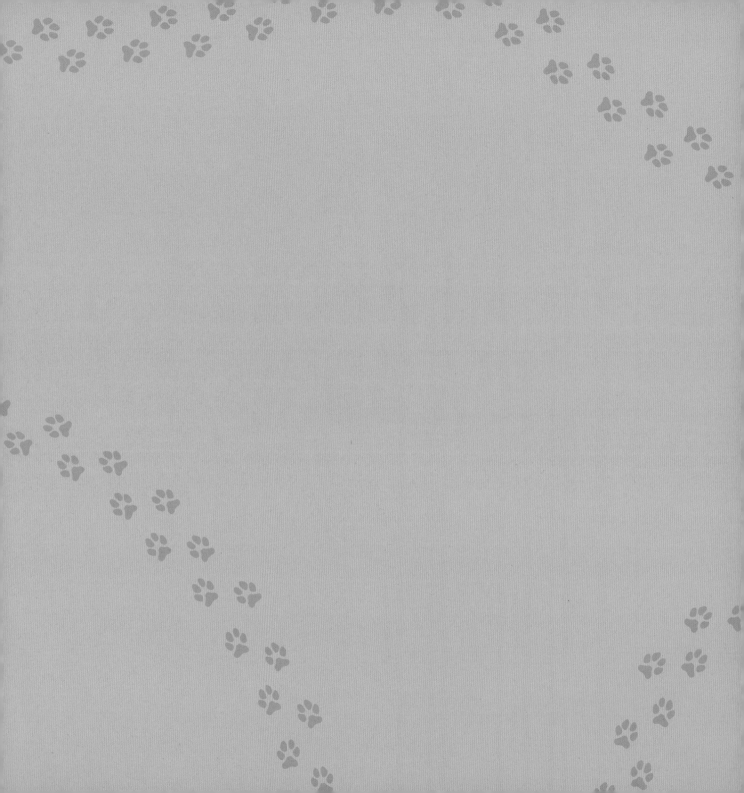

To Janet Eiby, who understands

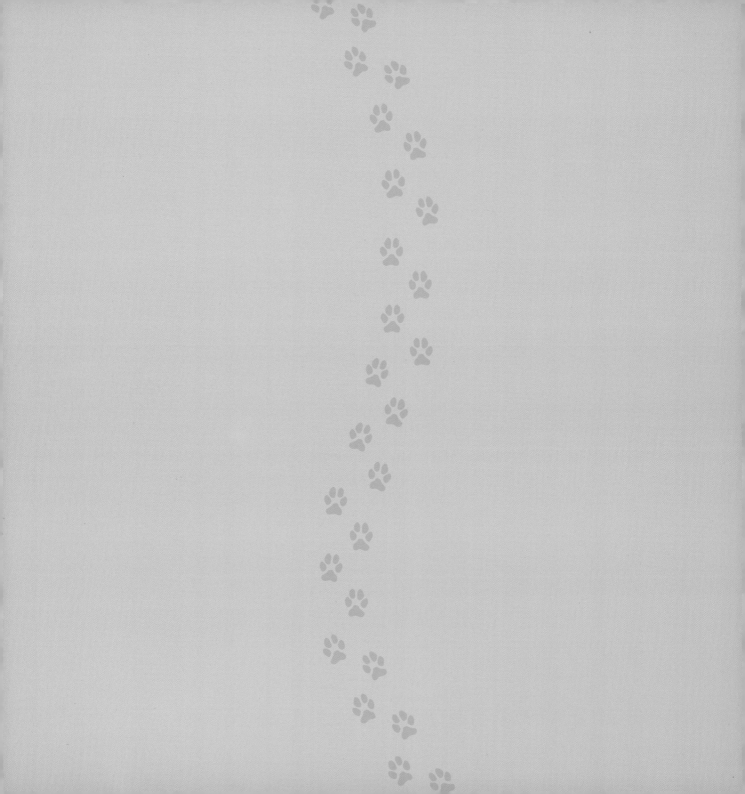

INTRODUCTION

Children on the Attention Deficit Hyperactivity Disorder (ADHD) spectrum can have challenges in three main areas:

1. They may find it hard to keep focused.
2. They may be hyperactive.
3. They may be impulsive.

Of course, anyone can find it hard to focus, or can be hyperactive or impulsive occasionally. The term ADHD is only used when these traits are exhibited so often that lives are disrupted.

But as you read, remember that not every child with ADHD has all the traits mentioned in this book. There are ADHD kids who are very active, and those who are not. Some may be outgoing, and others very shy. But all children with ADHD need understanding and love. They need specialist help, which may include medication and behaviour management.

Most of all, children with ADHD need people who believe in them, people to build their self-esteem, and people to go on life's journey with them, wherever it may lead.

Attention Deficit Hyperactivity Disorder
may be detected soon after birth.

Children with ADHD may not sleep as much as their parents would like.

Their first steps aren't steps...
they are an attempt to escape,

because the world is meant to be explored.

They know what they want and they want it NOW.

When an opportunity presents itself, they go for it,

and may dive straight into a situation without
thinking through the consequences.

Those with ADHD
can be fearless,

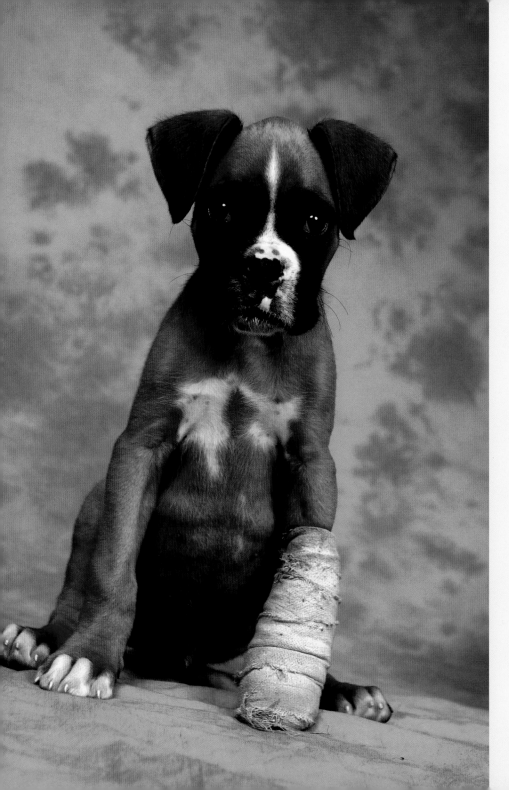

but unfortunately,
their bodies are
not so invincible.

They get lost easily,

they're always losing things,

"Is it down there?"

and often can't find what is right in front of their noses.

When playing, they may not be sure
how to take turns, or how to share,

and can be a bit rough at times.

They don't do this on purpose
and often feel bad about it later.

And yet, they have loving, caring natures,

and they can be so much fun!

Those with ADHD can be distracted
by things other people don't notice,

and their priorities may differ from those around them.

"But this is important!"

Their minds work better when their bodies are in motion and they find it hard to sit still for long.

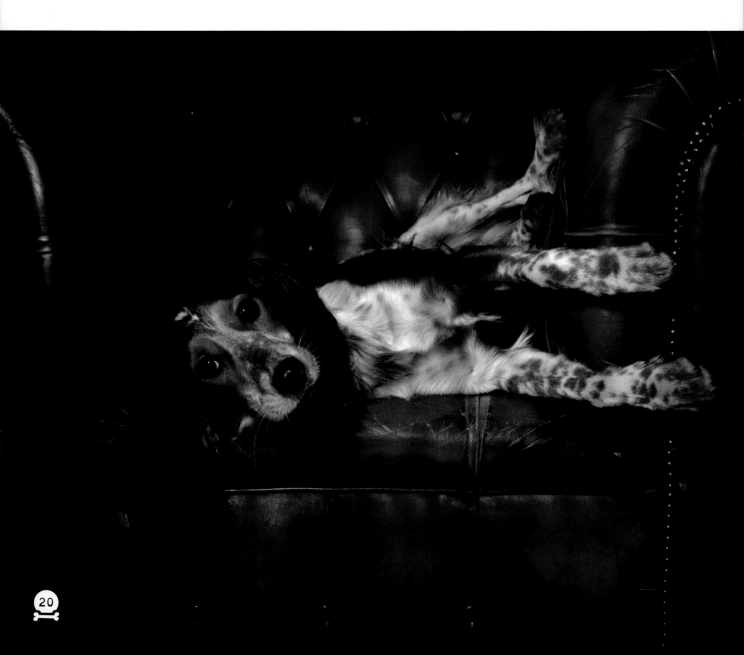

They are easily bored, and when that happens, their
brains fog and their eyes close all by themselves.

"Somewhere else" can seem
so much more interesting

and they dream of escaping to better things.

Their senses can get overloaded
with everything going on,

so they might dash from
one task to the next...

...without finishing anything.

They don't know where to start,

and even if there are instructions, they may not know how to follow them.

It's not that they can't learn things. They can!

But their brains don't always know how to retrieve the knowledge just learnt!

And there's no doubt
they are very bright,

but not everyone appreciates
their type of intelligence.

"I was just checking how
much it could bear."

So although they try hard to be good,

those in charge are
not always impressed
with their behaviour,

33

and they are often labeled as clowns.

Time can pass without them noticing,

"I'm supposed to be where? When?"

35

and they can end up in the doghouse
without knowing why.

People keep saying, "You can do better if you try harder," but it's simply not true.

Being very sensitive, they sometimes feel sad

because they want to be like everyone else,
but they just can't.

Life is so darn frustrating!

When things get too much,
they might have a meltdown.

Parents may not always understand their ADHD
children, but they still love them heaps.

Besides, the chances are, someone else in the family will behave exactly the same way.

When those with ADHD find something they like, their concentration is fierce,

and their dedication to the task is wholehearted.

Their minds work differently
from their peers.

They see the "big picture" easily,

and may find solutions where
others don't think to look.

Their creativity is legendary!

As children with ADHD grow older,
they can do anything they want,

and they are always willing
to try new things.

When life seems the same, day after day,

they know it's time for a change.

53

When they find a job they love,
their amazing sense of intuition,

their drive to achieve in their interest areas,

and their bright, inquisitive natures,

mean they can reach the
very top of their chosen field,

like many with ADHD before them.

Leonardo da Vinci

Jules Verne

Alexander Graham Bell

58

Sure, they may not worry about their looks, and
they have their own way of doing things,

but that's fine, because if everyone was the same, life would be very boring indeed.

When those with ADHD have love and support,

good friends who accept them just the way they are,

encouragement to
pursue their dreams,

and someone to believe in them,

their potential
is *limitless!*

65

Dog names and photograph credits

Cover image
Dalmatian © Bilevich Olga

page 1
Cocker Spaniel © Sergius4

page 2
Pinscher © Ann Tyurina

page 3
Welsh Corgi © Maria Ivanushkina

page 4
Shih Tzu © SM LIFESTYLE

page 5
Jack Russell Terrier © Javier Brosch

page 6
Mixed Breed © Shevs

page 7
Border Collie © xkunclova

page 8
Unnamed Breed © Enna8982

page 9
Boxer © Jan Quist

page 10
Jack Russell Terrier © Smit

page 11
German Shepherd © Anton Prokofev

page 12
Border Collie © Ksenia Raykova

page 13
Cross Breeds © Andrew Hagen

page 14
Staffordshire Terrier © Aleksey Boyko

page 15
Border Collie © Alexandra Morrison Photo

page 16
German Shepherd © Grigorita Ko

page 17
English Cocker Spaniel © Master1305

page 18
Husky © Enna8982

page 19
Siberian Husky © Vivienstock

page 20
Mixed Breed © Shevs

page 21
Brittany Spaniel © Kummeleon

page 22
Border Collie © OlgaOvcharenko

page 23
Beagle (not named by artist) © Sergey Nivens

page 24
Pit Bull Terrier © dezy

page 25
West Highland Terrier © Lopolo/rebeccaashworth/corners74

page 26
Jack Russell Terrier © sirtravelalot

page 27
Unnamed Breed © W. Scott McGill

page 28
Border Collie © StunningArt

page 29
Border Collie © StunningArt

page 30
Jack Russell Terrier © dezy

page 31
Jack Russell Terrier © dezy

page 32
Basset Hound © Annmarie Young

page 33
German Boxer and His Puppy © cynoclub

page 34
Chinese Crested Dog © Dora Zett

page 35
Siberian Husky © Seregraff

page 36
Unnamed Breed © Igor_83

page 37
Papillon © Alexandra Morrison Photo

page 38
American Staffordshire Terrier © Alex Zotov

page 39
Border Collie © Ksenia Raykova

page 40
Pug © fongleon356

page 41
Border Collie © Dale A Stork

page 42
Unnamed Breed © ValSN

page 43
Jack Russell Terrier and Nova Scotia Duck Tolling Retriever © dezy

page 44
Tibetan Mastiff Puppy © Agris Krusts

page 45
Havanese Dog © Bildagentur Zoonar GmbH

page 46
Laika Husky © Iryna Kalamurza

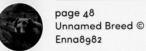
page 47
Siberian Husky © WICHAI WONGJONGJAIHAN

page 48
Unnamed Breed © Enna8982

page 49
Pointer © Barna Tanko

page 50
Akita Inu © BUY THIS

page 51
Jack Russell Terrier © Javier Brosch

page 52
Marble Dachshund © Anna.Ya

page 53
Yorkshire Terrier © anon_tae

page 54
Australian Shepherd © Alexandra Morrison Photo

page 55
Australian Shepherd © gpod

page 56
Toller Nova Scotia Duck Tolling Retriever © dezy

page 57
Afghan Hound © WildStrawberry

page 58
Mixed Breed/Jack Russell Terrier/Spitz-Dog © Ermolaev Alexander/dezy/Suponev Vladimir

page 59
Unnamed Breed © Karla Caspari

page 60
Irish Setter Puppies (from one nest) © De Jongh Photography

page 61
Siberian Husky Puppy and Mother © mariait

page 62
German Shepherd Puppies © DTeibe Photography

page 63
Mixed Breed © Enna8982

page 64
Border Collie Hugs Boxer Dog © Enna8982

page 65
Australian Shepherd Tricolor © dezy

First published in Great Britain in 2008 by Jessica Kingsley Publishers
Revised edition published in 2020 by Jessica Kingsley Publishers
An Hachette Company

1

Copyright © Kathy Hoopmann 2008, 2020

All photographs courtesy of Shutterstock.co.uk

A CIP catalogue record for this title is available from the British
Library and the Library of Congress

ISBN 978 1 78775 660 1
eISBN 978 1 78775 661 8

Printed and bound in China by Leo Paper Products

Jessica Kingsley Publishers' policy is to use papers that are natural,
renewable and recyclable products and made from wood grown
in sustainable forests. The logging and manufacturing processes
are expected to conform to the environmental regulations of the
country of origin.

Jessica Kingsley Publishers
73 Collier Street
London N1 9BE, UK

www.jkp.com

in the same series

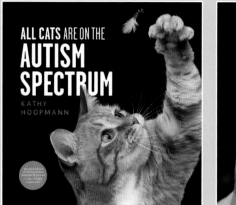

All Cats Are on the Autism Spectrum
Kathy Hoopmann
ISBN 978 1 78775 471 3
eISBN 978 1 78775 472 0

All Birds Have Anxiety
Kathy Hoopmann
ISBN 978 1 78592 182 7
eISBN 978 1 78450 454 0

by the same author

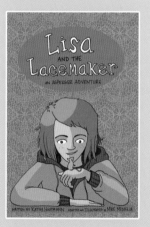

Lisa and the Lacemaker – The Graphic Novel
An Asperger Adventure
Kathy Hoopmann
Art and adaptation by Mike Medaglia
ISBN 978 1 78592 028 8
eISBN 978 1 78450 280 5

Blue Bottle Mystery – The Graphic Novel
An Asperger Adventure
Kathy Hoopmann
Art by Rachael Smith
ISBN 978 1 84905 650 2
eISBN 978 1 78450 204 1

Elemental Island
Kathy Hoopmann and J.S. Kiss
ISBN 978 1 84905 658 8
eISBN 978 1 78450 228 7